ABANDONED PLACES

SALTON RIVIERA

THE DESERTED RESORT COMMUNITY

DOOMED IN THE SEA

TORQUE

BY LISA OWINGS

TM

Torque brims with excitement
perfect for thrill-seekers of all kinds.
Discover daring survival skills, explore
uncharted worlds, and marvel at mighty
engines and extreme sports. In *Torque* books,
anything can happen. Are you ready?

This edition first published in 2020 by Bellwether Media, Inc.

Library of Congress Cataloging-in-Publication Data

Names: Owings, Lisa, author.
Title: Salton Riviera : the deserted resort community / by Lisa Owings.
Description: Minneapolis, MN : Bellwether Media, Inc., 2020. | Series:
Torque: abandoned places | Includes bibliographical references and
index. | Audience: Ages 7-12 | Audience: Grades 4-6 | Summary: "Amazing
photography accompanies engaging information about the Salton Riviera.
The combination of high-interest subject matter and light text is
intended for students in grades 3 through 7"– Provided by publisher
Provided by publisher.
Identifiers: LCCN 2019030421 | ISBN 9781644871638 (library binding) | ISBN
9781618918338 (ebook)
Subjects: LCSH: Tourism–California, Southern–Juvenile literature. |
Salton Sea (Calif.)–History–Juvenile literature.
Classification: LCC G155.U6 O95 2020 | DDC 979.4/99–dc23
LC record available at https://lccn.loc.gov/2019030421

Editor: Betsy Rathburn   Designer: Brittany McIntosh

Printed in the United States of America, North Mankato, MN. —

TABLE OF CONTENTS

NO SWIMMING

The stink of the Salton Sea hits you as you step out of the car. Your feet crunch over fish bones rotting in the desert sun. The water is thick with slime.

Getting Salty

The Salton Sea is about twice as salty as the ocean. It gets saltier every year.

graffiti

Yet this place has a haunting beauty.
Graffiti covers nearby buildings. Rusty cars
and boats dot the shore. Everything offers

Here and there, the Salton Riviera still harbors
signs of life. Flocks of birds soar overhead.
A few people explore the ruins.

East of the lake is an artist's paradise. Huge sculptures made of trash rise from the sand. A paint-covered mountain stands out in the dry desert. You move on, ready to leave this empty place.

Art with a Purpose

East Jesus is an artist community near the Salton Sea. Those who live there try to create no waste. They turn trash into art. They use the sun's energy to power their buildings!

PARADISE PAST

The Salton Riviera lies along the Salton Sea. This lake stretches over about 350 square miles (906 square kilometers) of desert in southern California. It sits in what used to be a dry, salt-crusted **basin**.

Salton Riviera,
California

N
W ✦ E
S

Flooding in 1905 caused the Colorado River
to overflow. It filled the basin, creating the
largest lake in California.

Salton Riviera
in the 1960s

People began to flock to this newly formed sea. By the 1950s, the Salton Riviera was one of the busiest vacation spots in California. Its beaches were crowded with people swimming, fishing, and soaking up the sun.

Fancy **resorts** hosted thousands of visitors each year. Now only their ruins remain. What happened to this desert paradise?

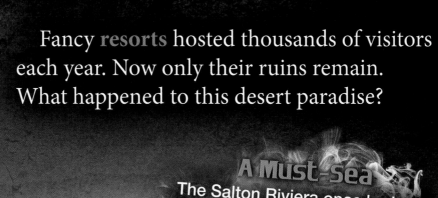

A Must-sea
The Salton Riviera once had more than 1.5 million visitors each year! It was busier than Yosemite, one of California's most popular national parks.

THE MIRACLE IN THE DESERT

In the 1900s, **canals** guided part of the Colorado River into the California desert. The water helped create rich farmland in the area.

Colorado River canal

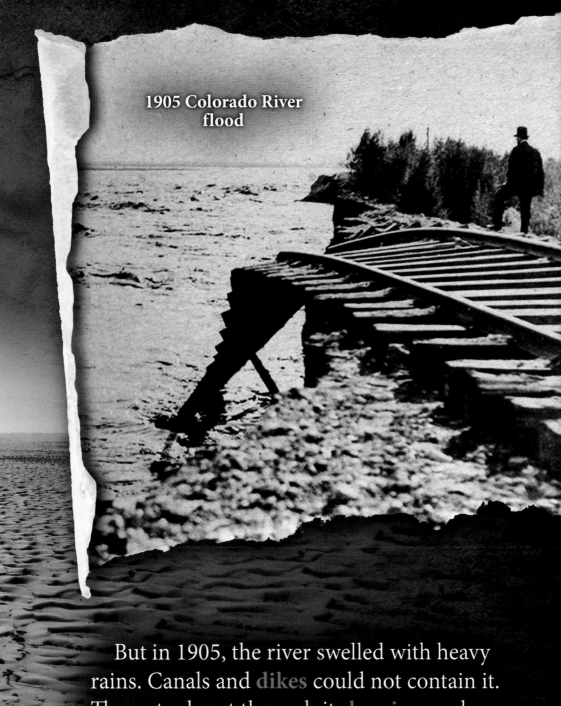

1905 Colorado River
flood

But in 1905, the river swelled with heavy
rains. Canals and dikes could not contain it.
The water burst through its barriers and
poured into the Salton Basin.

flood damage

Over the next 18 months, many tried and failed to stop the flood. The Southern Pacific Railroad finally succeeded in 1907.

But the basin had filled with river water. It had become the Salton Sea. Scientists thought the lake would dry up. When it did not, it was welcomed as a miracle in the desert.

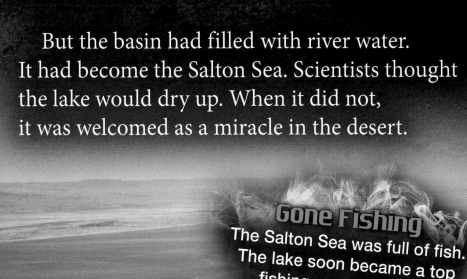

Gone Fishing

The Salton Sea was full of fish. The lake soon became a top fishing spot for people and birds!

At first, the lake mainly drew fishers. Between the 1920s and 1950s, several resorts sprouted up. Guests lounged on the beach or went boating. They hit the golf course or rolled up to a drive-in movie.

The lake was California's version of the French Riviera. But the lake's charm soon began to fade.

SALTON RIVIERA TIMELINE

1905:
Colorado River floods, creating Salton Sea

1950s:
Salton Sea resorts
draw millions of visitors

2007:
East Jesus community forms near Salton Sea

1970s:
Salt and pollution kill fish, cause odor, and drive away visitors

A DYING SEA

The Salton Riviera began to change in the 1970s. The Salton Sea was fed by runoff. Salt and chemicals from nearby farms poured in.

The sea was also drying up. The remaining water grew saltier and dirtier. Thousands of fish died, stinking up the beaches. Floods also hit the area. Damaged resorts never recovered.

Birds of the Salton Sea

The Salton Sea has been a protected area for birds since 1930. But by the 1990s, birds were dying by the thousands due to toxic waters and fish.

Tourists no longer wanted to visit the foul-smelling lake. Homes were abandoned. Boats and lounge chairs were left to rust on fish-bone beaches.

Every year, salt and pollution pose a bigger threat. These toxins may poison the air as the lake dries up. If the sea is not saved, even the birds may take flight and never return.

Saving the Sea

California hopes to turn the Salton Sea into a wetland bird habitat.

GLOSSARY

barriers—structures that prevent things or people from getting past them

basin—a bowl-shaped dip in Earth's surface; basins can be dry or filled with water.

canals—human-made waterways that allow water to flow from one area to another

dikes—walls or mounds built to hold back water and prevent flooding

French Riviera—a beautiful section of coast from southern France to northern Italy; the Riviera is famous for its pleasant climate and many resorts.

graffiti—writing or drawings put on public property without permission

paradise—a place of beauty and happiness

pollution—the introduction of materials that make things dirty or unsafe

resorts—places that offer vacationers a chance to rest and relax

ruins—the remains of human-made structures

runoff—water, usually from rain or melted snow, that flows over land and drains into other bodies of water; runoff picks up salt and toxins from polluted land along the way.

tourists—people who travel to visit another place

toxins—harmful materials

TO LEARN MORE

AT THE LIBRARY

Barnham, Kay. *The Great Big Water Cycle Adventure.* Hauppauge, N.Y.: Barrons Educational Series, Inc., 2018.

Blake, Kevin. *Salton Sea Resort: Death in the Desert.* New York, N.Y.: Bearport Publishing, 2015.

Labrecque, Ellen. *Clean Water.* Ann Arbor, Mich.: Cherry Lake Publishing, 2018.

ON THE WEB

FACTSURFER

Factsurfer.com gives you a safe, fun way to find more information.

1. Go to www.factsurfer.com.

2. Enter "Salton Riviera" into the search box and click 🔍.

3. Select your book cover to see a list of related web sites.

INDEX

The images in this book are reproduced through the courtesy of: Richard Wong/ Alamy, front cover; Scott London/ Alamy, p. 4; Michael Dwyer/ Alamy, p. 5; Matthew Dillon/ Flickr, pp. 6, 7, 8-9, 10, 20; MattLphotography, p. 11; National Geographic Image Collection/ Alamy, p. 12; Imperial Irrigation District, p. 13; Historic Images/ Alamy, p. 14; Tim Roberts Photography, p. 15; Ethan/ Flickr, pp. 16-17; Xinhua News Agency/ Getty Images, pp. 18-19; one5zero, p. 21.